You
Through
Him

Christianity's Identity Crisis

Rev, Dr. Georgette Joachim Milbin

Copyright © 2023 by Georgette Joachim Milbin

All rights reserved. No part of this book may be reproduced or transmitted in any form or by any means without written permission from the author.

ISBN 978: 1-7373227-5-7

You
Through
Him

Christianity's Identity Crisis

Dedication

This is dedicated to the **Holy Spirit,** to my husband, Abner Milbin, and my children Georabner, Georginio, Georvania, Geornipha, and Geornina. It is also in dedication to my amazing mother, Anna Andre, a strong woman. To my sisters: Michelle, Erline, Margaline, Ketely, Roseline, Jennipher, Gladys, and Naomie. To my Coach Betty Fortunat for *your guidance and support*, to all my church members in Haiti, Georgia, and the Dominican Republic.

CONTENTS

Foreword 1

Preface 5

Introduction: Who Am I? 7

Chapter One: Grand Theft 9

Chapter Two: Are We Honoring God With The
Respect He Deserves? 17

Chapter Three: Do You Know Who You Are? 25

Chapter Four: You Need To Know Who You Are In Christ 33

Chapter Five: Walk In Power With Your New Identity 37

Chapter Six: Our Identity Is In Christ 41

Chapter Seven: Discerning The Kingdom 47

Chapter Eight: The Veil Of Deception 59

Chapter Nine: You Judge Yourselves Unworthy 69

Chapter Ten: The Spirit Of Infirmity 73

Chapter Eleven: Recovering Our Sight 77

Chapter Twelve: Salvation, The Theme Of The Gospel 84

Chapter Thirteen: Ministers Of The Spirit 92

Now And Forever 102

Summary...114

About The Author...118

Sponsors..120

FOREWORD

Dr. Georgette Milbin is a pastor, a mother, a leader and great warrior that requires change wherever she goes in the Kingdom of God. She is an anointed vessel that God has raised up in this last hour to war against the principalities and powers of this world. A woman of God that is on a mission to retake territories that the enemy has captured, as she wars in the spirit of worship and praise.

Dr. Milbin is committed to God in every way, as she labors in the harvest fields both here in the United States and her native homeland Haiti. Souls are being saved as God uses her for His glory; hundreds have been touched and lives transformed as God uses her for His glory. She is truly a Proverbs 31 woman. Proverbs 31:10–31.

"Who can find a virtuous woman?" for her price is far above rubies. The heart of her husband doth safely trust in her, so that he shall have no need of spoil. She will do him good and not evil all the days of her life. She is like the merchant ships bringing her food from afar. She gets up while it is still dark; she provides food for her family and portions for her servant girls. She considers a field and buys it; out of her earnings she plants a vineyard. She sets about her work vigorously; her arms are strong for her tasks. She sees that her trading is profitable, and her lamp does not go out at night. In her hand she holds the distaff and grasps the spindle with her fingers. She opens her arms to the poor and extends her hands to the needy. When it snows, she has no fear for her household; for all of them are clothed in scarlet. She makes covering for her bed; she is clothed in fine linens and purple.

Her husband is respected at the city gate, where he takes his seat among the elders of the land. She makes linen garments and sells them and supplies the merchants with ashes. She is clothed with strength and dignity; she can laugh at the day to come. She speaks with wisdom, and faithful instruction is on her tongue. She watches over the affairs of her household and does not eat the bread of idleness. Her children arise and call her blessed; her husband also, and he praises her; many women do noble things, but you surpass them all. Charm is deceptive, and beauty is fleeting; but a woman who fears the LORD is to be praised. Give her the reward she has earned, and let her works bring her praise at the city gate." God bless you, Dr. Milbin, as you continue to do the will of the Lord until he comes.

Dr. Joan Williams

PREFACE

By reading this book, you will find your destiny by becoming who God creates you to be.

Too often, we feel pressured to define ourselves by what we can do: our jobs, financial status, successes, grades, appearance, what other people say about us, etc. Life is a journey full of surprises because we will experience failure, difficulties, and losses; we'll also be burned out in our jobs or places of service and people we wouldn't think will betray us.

Identity is not about you. We need to get out of the picture. Identity is how God sees us. In the Bible, there is a very special passage about identity. It is found in Ephesians 1:3-14. In this passage, the apostle Paul is writing to the Church in Ephesus. He explains that when we become Christians, we become new people with a new identity. According to Ephesians 1, when we are in

Christ, we have been blessed with every spiritual blessing. We have been chosen by God, adopted into His family, redeemed and forgiven. We have been given the gift of eternal life with God. Our identity in Christ can never be changed by anything we do.

Introduction

WHO AM I?

Let's define the new identity

Your identity is what you think of yourself and the things that make you unique. It is formed over the course of your life, from your experiences, relationships, culture, media, and the things around you. You're always shaping it in some way.

What is identity?

Your identity is what makes you who you are, the way you think about yourself, the way others see you, and the things that make you unique. Many people make New Year's Resolutions, such as trying to lose weight or going to bed at a certain time. Maybe you planned to exercise more, watch less television, or eat healthier, learn a new skill, or develop a closer walk with God. Well, we can say too bad; resolutions don't work.

More than 85 percent of people who set goals fail again. Let's say out loud that resolutions do not work.

Why can we say resolutions don't work?

Resolutions are usually just wishes that you think will happen. If you make a resolution because someone tells you to, you're probably going to have a hard time following through because you might not really want what you're saying you want or you might not be willing to do what it takes to make the resolution work. So it's a good idea to make resolutions that you actually want and are willing to work for. If you do not like the result, you need to change what you are doing.

Chapter One

GRAND THEFT

Jesus is introduced as the physical manifestation of God on Earth. This means that when people saw Him, they saw the Father. Jesus had the authority to teach and do the work of the Father because He was the Son of God. He showed mercy and compassion to people and He had the power to perform miracles like stopping the wind, raising Lazarus from the dead, and healing a man so he could walk. Satan challenged Jesus' right to be called the Son of God and the Pharisees called it blasphemy when Jesus said that He and the Father were one.

Jesus was always sure of Himself, never giving in to challenges. He called us to be like Him, walking in the same position and with the same authority. The same enemies that came against Jesus also come against us.

Satan challenges our right to be called children of God, and religion tells us that it is blasphemy to say that we are equal to or one with God.

God wants us to be like Him, to fill the role He created for us. He made us in His image, so that we could create things that are like Him. The right to walk as sons is rooted in God's plan for man.

Joh 1:12 But as many as received him, to them gave he power to become the sons of God, even to them that believe on his name:

Joh 1:13 Which were born, not of blood, nor of the will of the flesh, nor of the will of man, but of God.

Do you know who you are? Do you know what authority you have? Do you know where you come from and what your purpose is?

Colossians 2:10 Amp And you are in Him made full and having come to fullness of life [in Christ you too are filled with the godhead-Father, Son, and Holy Spirit and reach full spiritual stature].

Colossians 2:11 We are complete in Him.

Don't let someone else take control of your identity. You are who you are, and you will never let anyone else change that. When people see you, they will know that you are the Father.

John 17:22 And the glory which thou gave me I have given them; that they may be one, even as we are one:

John 17:23 I in them, and thou in me, that they may be made perfect in one; and that the world may know that thou hast sent me, and hast loved them, as thou hast loved me.

Identity was stolen SINCE THE Garden of Eden

Identity theft is when someone takes your personal information and uses it without your permission. This can be really scary because it means that someone could use your information to take control of your life, or even your money.

When we become Christians, we become part of a family that is special and loved by God. This family is linked to one another by the blood of Jesus Christ. When we trust in Him, He provides us with special protection so we can always be sure that we belong to Him.

Identity theft is a problem that has been happening for a long time, even though it is new. It is when someone's personal information is stolen and used without their permission. This can cause a lot of problems for the victim, like not being able to get benefits or services. In the Bible, the first recorded incident of identity theft happened in the Garden of Eden. Satan tricked Adam and Eve into eating from the Tree of Knowledge of Good and Evil, which led to their expulsion from the Garden of Eden. All over the Bible, every major figure struggled with understanding their own identity. For example, Satan tried to tempt Jesus twice by challenging His identity as the Son of God.

By accepting Christ as our Savior, the Bible tells us:

1- As Christians, we are new creations in Christ (see 2 Corinthians 5:17)

2- We are children of God, heirs of God, and fellow heirs with Christ. We share His inheritance and have His nature and love in us (see Romans 8:17; 1 John 4:6–8)

3- We are not alone; the Holy Spirit lives in us and helps us to comfort, teach, and guide us. He also intercedes for us and strengthens us (see John 14:16–17)

4- We have all of God's fullness and every spiritual blessing in us (see John 1:16)

5- We have received from our heavenly Father every spiritual blessing in heavenly places in Christ who is in us (see Ephesians 1:3)

6- Having a spirit of power, love, and a well-balanced, disciplined mind helps us to have the mind, thoughts, and feelings of Christ (see 2 Timothy 1:7)

7- Having the grace of Christ helps us to have the strength and power we need to follow His will for our lives. We need to renew our minds daily so that we stay in agreement with God's Word (see 1 Corinthians 2:16)

8- This helps us to have the mind, thoughts, and feelings He desires for us (see 2 Corinthians 12:7–9)

9- We must renew our minds daily to align with the Word of God, which is also the will of God for our lives (see Romans 12:2)

10- We can rely on, trust in, and be confident in our relationship with God, His Word, His promises, and His love for us (see Proverbs 3:5–6)

11- To everyone who received Him, He gave the right to become children of God (see John 1:12)

For example, Jesus said in John 10:10 that the thief comes only to steal and kill and destroy. But on the cross, Jesus said it was finished. He completed His part in restoring abundance, wholeness, healing, deliverance, success, prosperity, victory, grace, love, and truth to those who believe in Him and His Word. He brought heaven back to Earth in Christ. With Christ, your identity is always safe, and secure, and never needs to be reset. What is the password? It's easy and simple to remember: JESUS DID IT ALL! IT IS DONE. JESUS DID IT ALL!

Application and Reflection

Keeping your identity in Christ is important because He will keep you safe and secure. Remember that Jesus did everything for us and we can trust Him to keep us in perfect peace. We can do this by believing what the Bible says about us and then living our lives by faith in what

He has done. We should also praise God at all times and give Him thanks for all He has done for us.

1- **Believe** in God and His Word
2- **Accept** the work of Jesus Christ at the cross
3- **Submit** yourself to the Lord
4- **Be** a living sacrifice
5- **Renew** your mind
6- **Fast** and **pray** and **read** the Word of God.

Chapter Two

ARE WE HONORING GOD WITH THE RESPECT HE DESERVES?

We sing songs of praise to God, Jesus, and others in order to give honor and glory to them. We try to serve Him faithfully, but we often have trouble giving Him the credit He deserves. The Pharisees respected God with their words, but their hearts were far from Him. They knew about their sin, and that kept them from being close to God.

Isaiah 29:13 Wherefore the Lord said, Forasmuch as this people draw near me with their mouth, and with their lips do honor me, but have removed their heart far from me, and their fear toward me is taught by the precept of men:

Isaiah felt the same way when he found himself in the presence of God. "Who am I in the presence of God?" **Isaiah 6:1-7** We often feel the same way even though we have been forgiven.

***Colossians 1:21** And you, that were sometime alienated and enemies in your mind by wicked works, yet now hath he reconciled. **22** In the body of his flesh through death, to present you holy and unblameable and unreproveable in his sight:*

Jesus died for our sins so that we could walk in our inheritance. **Psalms 106:4-5,20** He exchanged his life for ours and called us joint heirs. **Galatians 4:1-7**

Just what does that mean? Until we begin to understand what our inheritance involves, we have missed the whole point. Our hearts are still far from Him. God wants us to fully assume and walk in our inheritance. Until we do that, we are not really giving God the credit due His name. **James 3:9-10**

Jesus was the first-born among many brethren. He was appointed heir of all things. He was the express image of his father. **Hebrews 1:2-3** He was different than the angels. He inherited a more excellent name. He inherited all of the rights and privileges that go with being his Father's son, including the throne.

Hebrews 1:4 *Being made so much better than the angels, as he hath by inheritance obtained a more excellent name than they.*

5 For unto which of the angels said he at any time, Thou art my Son, this day have I begotten thee? And again, I will be to him a Father, and he shall be to me a Son?

8 But unto the Son he saith, Thy throne, O God, is for ever and ever: a scepter of righteousness is the scepter of thy kingdom.

The angels were created to be ministering spirits that minister to the saints and to the Father. They surround the throne and cry, "Holy, holy, holy." Yet, they were never created to inherit the things of the throne and of the Kingdom. They are not heirs. **Hebrews 1:5,713-14**

Mankind was created to be an heir. **Genesis 1:26-28** The position has been secured for us by Jesus. Jesus shared His glory with us and is not ashamed to call us brothers. **Hebrews 2:9-12** Can you picture yourself seated in heavenly places sharing the Father's glory and honor like Jesus did? **Ephesians 2:5-6**

If you can't, then you are not fully receiving the position Jesus secured for you. **John 1:12-13,16** For the most part, we agree that Jesus died for our sins, but we have never dared to fully assume our position as a joint heir. We have almost adopted the position of angels. We give Him glory and honor and we work for the Kingdom, but we cannot picture ourselves seated in heavenly places occupying the throne.

***Psalms 100:4** Enter into his gates with thanksgiving, and into his courts with praise: be thankful unto him, and bless his name.*

***Psalms 96:8** Give unto the LORD the glory due unto his name: bring an offering, and come into his courts.*

Unless we believe that Jesus has paid the price for our sins so we can be like HIM, we are only paying lip service to God.

God is the one who is able to provide the best life possible for His children, and He won't share His glory with anyone else. But as a father, He is willing to share everything he has with his kids. He provides us with his fullness, and we should never miss it. Take your rightful position as a son and joint heir. Jesus did! YOU CAN TOO

I am not saying we are God. I want you to know that Jesus said we are one with God, we can do even greater things than these, because I am going to the Father. **See John 14:12**

We are one with God. If we try to assume the position outside of being one with him, then we are exalting we must Pray

Jesus instructed in His model prayer that our prayers should begin with hallowing God's name (Matt. 6:9). An elder friend recommends leading off with, "I love you, Father!" I like to continue with, "I love Jesus Christ, your Son! I love your Church! I love your Work! I love your Bible! I love your way! And please give me more of your love!"

Our daily lives should begin this way too—days are better when they begin with thanking God for a new day (Psa. 55:17). Of course, David says it's good to also pray daily at noon and in the evening.

David said, "Oh, magnify the Lord with me, and let us exalt His name together" (Psa. 34:3). Some Bibles have supplementary material giving two or more pages of names, titles and offices for Jesus Christ. Beware the "sacred name" heresy—God has many names.

Think YHVH Ropha as you pray about your long list of people needing healing. Think of Elohim and be grateful God is calling you to His Family. Think of Jesus Christ who is your Savior. Take time to learn God's many names, titles and offices. My favorite is to thank God daily that the supreme power of the universe is good, giving, kind—and glorious!

Keep God's Commandments. We say we love God. The first four Commandments are how God says we actually give love to Him. Are we really keeping them? "For this is the love of God, that we keep His commandments" (1 John 5:3).

Give God the respect due His name

Not doing this cost Moses the physical Promised Land (Num. 20:8–12). All the complainers finally got to him so that he struck the rock twice instead of just speaking to it like he did the last time. Bad as that was, he then shouted, "Hear now, you rebels! Must *we* bring water for you out of this rock?" Actually Moses and Aaron were the real rebels! Why does it usually turn out that we accuse when we're guilty of the same? Because all sin is common to man and one of the most common is accusing!

God chastised Moses severely. "Because you did not believe Me, to hallow Me in the eyes of the children of Israel." Perhaps Moses and Aaron lapsed into thinking their closeness to God and being His leaders gave them some license. Yet God holds His leaders to stricter accountability (James 3:1). And we are never too old to be tested.

Yet God is so merciful. God still brought forth the water they needed. Moses will still be in the better Promised Land.

Choose good music and entertainment

"I will praise the name of God with a song" (Psa. 69:30).

I love the song "Today" by John Denver, which has the astute line: "You'll know who I am by the songs that I sing." And by what we read and by which movies we watch. The rating we should be concerned with is God's! Are we busy decrying the sex and violence on *our* TV?

Check God's advice in Eph. 5:18–19 and Col. 3:16–17. Good spiritual songs can provide not only beautiful music to inspire us but beautiful thoughts that point us to honoring God.

Honor Jesus Christ

The Father has given his Son "the name which is above every name." At that name every knee, no matter how skinned or even broken it has to suffer, will bow to Him. "Every tongue."

Chapter Three

DO YOU KNOW WHO YOU ARE?

Jesus knew who He was. His identity was continually challenged by the enemy through the religious leaders of the day. He was not moved. He knew who He was, He knew what He came to do, and He knew where He was going.

John 13:3 *Jesus knowing that the Father had given all things into his hands, and that he was come from God, and went to God;*

Jesus never saw himself separated from His Father and He was secure in the relationship that He had with Him.

John 8:29 *And he that sent me is with me: the Father hath not left me alone; for I always do those things that please him.*

Jesus embraced who He was.

Mat 7:28 *And it came to pass, when Jesus had ended these sayings, the people were astonished at his doctrine:*

Mat 7:29 For he taught them as one having authority, and not as the scribes.

Jesus was filled with the same glory and honor that His Father was filled with.

Colossians 2:9 Amp *For in Him the whole fullness of Deity [the Godhead] continues to dwell in bodily form [giving complete expression of the divine nature].*

He was a perfect manifestation of His Father.

Heb 1:2-7 *Hath in these last days spoken unto us by his Son, whom he hath appointed heir of all things, by whom also he made the worlds;*

Heb 1:3 *Who being the brightness of his glory, and the express image of his person, and upholding all things by the word of his power. . . .*

He inherited the throne!

Heb 1:8 *But unto the Son he saith, Thy throne, O God, is for ever and ever: a scepter of righteousness is the scepter of thy kingdom.*

He and His Father were one.

Joh 1:1 *In the beginning was the Word, and the Word was with God, and the Word was God.*

Do we know who we are?

Jesus exchanged His life for ours. **Romans 6:1–5** He exchanged His glory and honor for our shame and weakness. **2 Corinthians 5:21**

2Th 2:13 *But we are bound to give thanks always to God for you, brethren beloved of the Lord, because God hath from the beginning chosen you to salvation through sanctification of the Spirit and belief of the truth:*

2Th 2:14 Whereunto he called you by our gospel, to the obtaining of the glory of our Lord Jesus Christ.

As we have borne the image of the earthly, we will also bear the image of the heavenly.

1Co 15:45 *And so it is written, The first Adam was made a living soul; the last Adam was made a quickening spirit.*

1Co 15:46 Howbeit that was not first which is spiritual, but that which is natural; and afterward that which is spiritual.

1Co 15:47 <u>The first man is</u> of the earth<u>, earthy</u>: <u>the second man is the Lord from heaven.</u>

1Co 15:48 As is the earthy, such are they also that are earthy: and <u>as is the heavenly, such are they also that are heavenly.</u>

1Co 15:49 And as we have borne the image of the earthy, <u>we shall</u> also <u>bear the image of the heavenly.</u>

We are full of the same honor and glory that Jesus is filled with.

Joh 17:22 *And <u>the glory which thou gave me I have given them</u>; that they may be one, even as we are one:*

He gave us the power and the right to be sons of God. He filled us with His fullness! He gave us everything He had.

Joh 1:12 *But as many as received him, to them gave he power to become the sons of God, even to them that believe on his name:*

Joh 1:13 *Which were born, not of blood, nor of the will of the flesh, nor of the will of man, but of God.*

Joh 1:14 *And the Word was made flesh, and dwelt among us, (and <u>we beheld his glory, the glory as of the only begotten of the Father,) full of grace and truth.</u>*

Joh 1:16 *And <u>of his fullness</u> **[all that he is filled with]** <u>have all we received</u>, and grace for grace.*

We came from the Father, and we are going back to Him.

Eph 1:4 *According as he hath chosen us in him before the foundation of the world, that we should be holy and without blame before him in love:*

Ecc 12:7 *Then shall the dust return to the earth as it was: and the spirit shall return unto God who gave it.*

We are heirs of the Kingdom and of the throne. An heir inherits everything that belonged to his predecessor and assumes his position.

Gal 4:4 *But when the fullness of the time was come, God sent forth his Son, made of a woman, made under the law,*

Gal 4:5 To redeem them that were under the law, that we might receive the adoption of sons.

Gal 4:6 And because ye are sons, God hath sent forth the Spirit of his Son into your hearts, crying, Abba, Father.

Gal 4:7 Wherefore thou art <u>no more a servant, but a son</u>; and if a son, then <u>an heir of God through Christ.</u>

Let this mind be in you which was also in Christ Jesus:

Php 2:5 *Let this mind be in you, which was also in Christ Jesus:*

Php 2:6 *Who, <u>being in the form of God</u>, <u>thought it not robbery to be equal with God</u>:*

Php 2:7 *But made himself of no reputation, and took upon him the form of a servant, and was made in the likeness of men:*

We were made in the image of God. We have a body of flesh, but we have been filled with His Spirit for the purpose of demonstrating the "person of God" to mankind.

Colossians 2:10 Amp *and <u>you are in Him</u> made full and <u>having come to fullness</u> of life [in Christ you too are filled with the godhead-Father, Son and Holy Spirit and reach full spiritual stature].*

Colossians 2:11 Amp <u>*We are complete in Him.*</u>

Jesus was the Word made flesh and we are flesh filled with the Word. We are incorruptible.

1Pe 1:23 *Being <u>born again</u>, not of corruptible seed, but of incorruptible, <u>by the word of God</u>, which liveth and abideth forever.*

1Pe 1:24 For all flesh is as grass, and all the glory of man as the flower of grass. The grass withereth, and the flower thereof falleth away:

1Pe 1:25 But <u>the word of the Lord endureth forever</u>. And this is the word which by the gospel is preached unto you.

Chapter Four

YOU NEED TO KNOW WHO YOU ARE IN CHRIST

In order to be a good Christian, you need to know your identity in Christ. This means understanding who you are, what your purpose in life is, and how to best follow Jesus.

If you feel like you're always losing and you don't have any confidence that can really hold you back in life. But if you know who you are in Christ, you can face anything with confidence. Life is a puzzle; we must put each piece where it belongs to reach our destiny. We can only do it by knowing who we are in Christ- because we have an enemy, like John 10:10, whose mission is to kill, steal and destroy. We must submit ourselves to the Lord Jesus Christ. He can reveal to us the enemy's plan.

Now we can change from an insecure person to a woman who knows her position and divine purpose in Christ.

The key to overcoming obstacles in life starts with knowing who you really are—the person you are in Christ.

Jesus had a conversation with His disciples about personality in Matthew 13. He asked, "Who do people think I am?" The disciples answered who others thought Jesus was. Then Jesus asked, "Who do you say I am?"

Simon famously replied, "You are the Christ, the Son of the Living God."

Now Jesus explains to them, "You are Peter, and on this rock I will build My church and it will change the world."

Now I have a question for you: who is Christ to you?

Is Jesus just a good man? No, He is much more than that. He is a prophet, a historical figure, and the Savior of the world. He died for our sins and rose again to give us eternal life. Knowing who you are starts with getting to know Him better each day.

The key is to get to know Jesus for who He really is, not just how others see Him. Some people might see Jesus as a stern judge, but He's actually the opposite. He's a loving God who is full of mercy and grace. He's slow to anger and He won't punish you for your mistakes.

Who you are comes from knowing who Jesus is.

Peter realized who he really was and what he was meant to do when he accepted Jesus as the Christ. Before that, he was just Simon, a fisherman. Even though he followed Jesus, his life didn't have much purpose. But once he acknowledged Jesus as the Christ, everything changed. He became known as Peter, the strong foundation that Jesus could build His Church on.

Identity is found in getting to know Jesus better and understanding how much He loves you. Knowing how valuable you are to Him and that He has made you righteous contributes to your identity. When you know how much God loves you and how He has set you free, you can't help but be strong and stay true to yourself.

When you know who you are through Christ, you will be able to fulfill your destiny

Once Peter realized who he really was in Christ, he went from being an ordinary fisherman to a Christian with authority and power. On the day of Pentecost, he preached and thousands of people were saved. He performed miracles and is credited as the founder of the Church. Jesus' prophecy was fulfilled—Peter changed the world. But it was not the man, it was the revelation. Peter found out who he was in Christ, and it made all the difference.

Read, meditate, dig into the Word, and search Scripture to discover Christ—not just who others deem Him to be, but as He is. Then look for "in Christ" passages that reveal your authority and righteousness.

"For no matter how many promises God has made, they are 'Yes' in Christ. And so through him the 'Amen' is spoken by us to the glory of God." 2 Corinthians 1:20

All the promises of God in Christ are yes. That means the sky is the limit. Who and what's stopping you walking toward your victory in Christ? Just like Peter, when you know who you are in Christ, you will change the world and yourself.

Chapter Five

WALK IN POWER WITH YOUR NEW IDENTITY

Jesus is all-powerful, and His power can help us overcome anything. We don't need to do anything to win a battle; we just need to rely on Him. He showed us how powerful He is when He rose from the dead, conquering death. We have the same power through the Holy Spirit. Knowing this truth allows us to be confident in who we are.

Knowing that you are loved by God gives you the confidence to be who you are meant to be, no matter what anyone else says or does. You have the power of the Holy Spirit to help you stay strong in your identity.

There is a power that is always available to you and that can't be stopped by anything. This power is Jesus.

When you call on Him, you know that the Spirit is in you. You can remind yourself of this power by reading the Book of Acts. Jesus' power is in you and is undefeated because He conquered it all.

The Bible is powerful because it is not just a book with words, but the words in it have a lot of power. The Bible can help us understand what God is like and how we should live. The Bible is like a heart because it can help you figure out when you're thinking lies about yourself and show you the truth instead. If you think about the Bible a lot, it can change your heart and mind so that you live according to the truth of who you are.

You can trust what God says about you. It's important to think about what His Word says every day. This takes faith and effort.

The power of knowing who you are in Christ comes from His Word. His Word is more powerful than any lie the enemy might tell you, because it is the truth.

1- He will help you stay true to yourself. When you trust Jesus, you can be sure that He will always help you and never let you down

   When we trust someone, it means that we know they will take care of whatever we give them. We shouldn't feel overwhelmed or stressed about it because that's when the enemy can take advantage of us.

2- Remember how much God loves you and that He wants to take care of everything for you. The enemy wants you to find your identity in the world instead of in Christ. But you can trust that Jesus is all-powerful and His Word is true. This means you are completely free. He can do it, so trust Him and relax in his presence.

Chapter Six

OUR IDENTITY IS IN CHRIST

Do you want to know how awesome your life can be in Christ? Let's review some of the things that God says about you and how He wants you to live. Say them out loud with me!

I am complete in Jesus, who is the head over all rule and authority—of every angelic and earthly power (Colossians 2:10).

I am living with Jesus Christ (Ephesians 2:5).

I am no longer controlled by the law of sin and death (Romans 8:2).

I will not live in fear of oppression (Isaiah 54:14).

I am a child of God, and the evil one cannot hurt me (1 John 5:18).

I am holy and without blame before Him in love (Ephesians 1:4; 1 Peter 1:16).

I think like Christ does (1 Corinthians 2:16; Philippians 2:5).

I have a peace from God that is stronger than anything else (Philippians 4:7).

The Spirit of God is more powerful than the enemy and lives inside me (1 John 4:4).

I have received a lot of grace from Jesus Christ, and because of that I am able to live a life full of righteousness (Romans 5:17).

I have received the Spirit of wisdom and revelation in the knowledge of Jesus, which has enlightened the eyes of my heart, so that I know the hope of having life in Christ (Ephesians 1:17–18).

I have received the power of the Holy Spirit, which means that I can do miraculous things. I have authority over the enemy in this world, which means that I can defeat them (Mark 16:17–18; Luke 10:17–19).

I am reborn in my understanding of God, and I no longer want to live like I did before I became a Christian (Colossians 3:9–10).

I am kind and forgiving, and I don't judge others. I do this because God is merciful and forgiving, and He blesses me when I live like this (Luke 6:36–38).

God gives me everything I need, based on His great riches in Christ Jesus (Philippians 4:19).

I always have faith in God, and this helps me to resist any attacks from my enemies (Ephesians 6:16).

I can do whatever I need to do in life through Christ Jesus who gives me strength (Philippians 4:13).

I can do anything I need to do in life, because Christ Jesus gives me the strength to do it (1 Peter 2:9).

I have been spiritually transformed and renewed by the living and everlasting Word of God, and I am now set apart for His purpose (1 Peter 1:23).

I am God's handiwork, created in Christ to do good deeds that He has prepared for me to do (Ephesians 2:10).

I am a brand-new person in Christ (2 Corinthians 5:17).

In Christ, I am no longer controlled by sin—my relationship to it is broken—and I am now controlled by

God—living in unbroken fellowship with Him (Romans 6:11).

The light of God's truth has filled my heart and given me knowledge of salvation through Christ (2 Corinthians 4:6).

I am blessed when I do what God's Word says (James 1:22, 25).

I am a part of what God has promised to Christ, and I will receive the same inheritance as Christ (Romans 8:17).

I am more than a conqueror through Him who loves me (Romans 8:37).

I overcome the enemy of my soul by the blood of the Lamb and the word of my testimony (Revelation 12:11).

I have everything I need to live a godly life and am equipped to live in His divine nature. This means that I am able to live according to God's will and nature, and not my own (2 Peter 1:3–4).

I am a follower of Christ who helps others learn about Him (2 Corinthians 5:20). I am part of a generation that was chosen by God, a royal priesthood that belongs to God, a holy nation that is set apart for God, and a people who have been purchased by God (1 Peter 2:9).

I have a good relationship with God because of what Jesus did (2 Corinthians 5:21).

My body is a place where the Holy Spirit lives; I am His property (1 Corinthians 6:19).

I am in charge of my life and I always make choices that lead me to a better life because I trust and obey God (Deuteronomy 28:13).

I am a source of light and hope for the world (Matthew 5:14).

I am chosen by God and forgiven through Christ. I have a compassionate heart, kindness, humility, meekness and patience (Romans 8:33; Colossians 3:12).

I am forgiven by God because of what Jesus did on the cross. His blood cleanses me from all sin (Ephesians 1:7).

I have been saved from the evil forces of darkness and brought into God's good kingdom (Colossians 1:13).

I am free from the punishment of sin, sickness, and poverty (Deuteronomy 28:15-68; Galatians 3:13).

I believe in Jesus and am so thankful for everything He has done for me (Colossians 2:7).

I am very grateful to God for everything He has done for me. My life is based on my trust in Him, and I am constantly thanking Him for His blessings (Psalm 66:8; 2 Timothy 1:9).

I am healed and whole because of what Jesus did for me (Isaiah 53:5; 1 Peter 2:24).

I am saved by God's grace. I am raised up with Christ and seated with Him in heavenly places (Ephesians 2:5–6; Colossians 2:12).

God loves me very much (John 3:16; Ephesians 2:4; Colossians 3:12; 1 Thessalonians 1:4).

I have been given all the strength I need by God, who is full of glory and might. (Colossians 1:11).

I ask God for help, and the devil goes away because I say "no" to him in Jesus' name. (James 4:7).

I am not afraid of anything because the Holy Spirit lives inside me and gives me His power, love and self-control (2 Timothy 1:7).

Christ lives inside me, and I live by trusting in Him and His love for me. (Galatians 2:20).

Chapter Seven

DISCERNING THE KINGDOM

The things of the kingdom can only be spiritually discerned.

1 Corinthians 2:9–14

1Co 2:14 But the natural man received not the things of the Spirit of God: for they are foolishness unto him: neither can he know them, because they are spiritually discerned.

1 Corinthians 15:34–50 tells us that the things that pertain to the flesh and the things that pertain to the Spirit are not the same because they are opposites. They do not function the same way. They cannot be mixed.

We have tried to make the things of the kingdom about the things of the flesh and we have missed the whole point!

1Co 15:50 Now this I say, brethren, that flesh and blood cannot inherit the kingdom of God; neither do corruption inherit incorruption.

The Kingdom is not about rules and regulations. It is a spiritual Kingdom, not a flesh kingdom.

Rom 14:17 For the kingdom of God is not meat and drink; but righteousness, and peace, and joy in the Holy Ghost.

The Kingdom is not something that you can see with your eyes or enter with your body. It is something that you can only know about if the Holy Spirit reveals it to you. Unless you are born again, you cannot understand or enter the Kingdom. You will never be able to understand or experience righteousness, peace, and joy. This is because you are limited by your physical body and cannot perceive spiritual things.   John 3:1-5

The enemy is trying to trick us by appealing to our fleshly desires, which are corrupt and have no spiritual value. This way, our understanding of what is spiritual becomes distorted.

Col 2:8 Beware lest any man spoil [rob] you through philosophy and vain deceit, after the tradition of men, after the rudiments of the world, and not after Christ.

Many Christians get frustrated because they don't understand this concept.

Jas 1:8 A double minded man is unstable in all his ways.

How do you know what you know about God? Do you have knowledge that comes from hearing stories passed down from other people (tradition), as well as from what you have read or been taught (head knowledge), mixed with knowledge that comes from God Himself (revelation knowledge)?

Proverbs 4:7 NIV... though it costs all you have, get understanding.

If we want to understand what God is like, we should ask the Holy Spirit for help. We might find out that what we thought we knew about God isn't true. But if we're willing to let go of our old ideas and question religious traditions, we can find the truth about God, and it will set us free!

Eph 1:17 That the God of our Lord Jesus Christ, the Father of glory, may give unto you the spirit of wisdom and revelation in the knowledge of him:

Eph 1:18 The eyes of your understanding being enlightened; <u>that ye may know what is the hope of his calling, and what the riches of the glory of his inheritance in the saints</u>,

Eph 1:19 And <u>what is the exceeding greatness of his power to us-ward</u> who believe, <u>according to the working of his mighty power.</u>

We are His workmanship!

Eph 2:8 For by grace [Strong's – the divine influence of God in your life and its reflection therein] are ye saved through faith [persuasion that He will provide everything that you need]; and that not of yourselves: it is the gift of God:

Eph 2:9 Not of works, lest any man should boast.

Eph 2:10 For we are his workmanship, created in Christ Jesus unto good works, which God hath before ordained that we should walk in them.

Where is the Kingdom of God?

The Kingdom is not only in your heart. Christ's statement that "the Kingdom of God is within you" is a poor translation from the original Greek and can be translated "the Kingdom of God is among you." Closer inspection reveals He was actually referring to Himself as a representative of that Kingdom.

Jesus said that the Kingdom of God is inside each one of us

Jesus was saying that He is the King of the coming Kingdom of God, and He was standing in the midst of His def....

"The kingdom of God is within you," Bible verse

Responding to a question from the Pharisees about when the Kingdom of God would come, Jesus said, "The kingdom of God does not come with observation; nor will they say, 'See here!' or 'See there!' For indeed, *the kingdom of God is within you*" (Luke 17:20–21).

"The kingdom of God is within you" meaning

The first sentence of Jesus' answer has been fairly easy to understand. Misunderstanding regarding the second sentence, however, has given many an incomplete picture of the Kingdom.

When Jesus came to earth, the Jews were looking for the Messiah to come and elevate the Jewish nation to prominence. Instead of hearing a message of repentance, they anticipated a Deliverer who would lead them in a successful liberation of their nation. And some of the religious authorities apparently believed that they—because of their careful investigation—would be the ones to first discover the promised Savior's coming.

In the above-noted passage, Jesus told the Pharisees that their thinking was mistaken. Jesus' first coming was to preach "the gospel of the kingdom of God" (Mark 1:14–15) and pay the penalty for mankind's sins. Later, He would "appear a second time ... for salvation" (Hebrews 9:28) and the establishment of the Kingdom of God here on Earth.

Jesus made this same point when He was on trial before Pilate. When asked if He was the King of the Jews, Jesus answered, "My kingdom is not of this world. If My kingdom were of this world, My servants would fight, so that I should not be delivered to the Jews; but now My kingdom is not from here" (John 18:36).

How Jesus said the Kingdom of God would come

When Jesus returns, there will indeed be dramatic signs that all will be able to discern (Matthew 24:5-14, 21–27; Revelation 1:7). But in saying, "The kingdom of God does not come with observation; nor will they say, 'See here!' or 'See there!'" (Luke 17:20–21), Jesus was explaining to the Pharisees of that generation that, in spite of their meticulous efforts, their mistaken understanding would not allow them to identify the Messiah's first coming.

Furthermore, they would not see the astonishing signs of His second coming—the signs for which they were looking. As Jesus noted, His second coming would be in another "day" (verse 24)—a time period long after the Pharisees to whom He was speaking had lived and died.

After telling the Pharisees that they wouldn't be able to observe the coming of the Kingdom of God in the way they had anticipated, He said, "For indeed, the kingdom of God is within you" (verse 21).

In this sense, Jesus, the King of the coming Kingdom of God, was standing in the midst of the Pharisees. In this passage, *entos* (the Greek word that is translated "within") can also be translated "in the midst of" (*Vine's Complete Expository Dictionary of Old and New Testament Words*). The New American Standard Bible, the New International Version, the Modern King James Version and Green's Literal Translation translate this phrase as "in your midst."

In this sense, Jesus, the King of the coming Kingdom of God, was standing in the midst of the Pharisees. These translations are clearly better, for the Kingdom of God was not in the hearts of these Pharisees.

(For more help understanding the Kingdom of God, see our article "What Is the Kingdom of God?")

Is the Kingdom of God in our hearts?

So what about the concept of the Kingdom of God being in our hearts? It certainly was not in the hearts of the Pharisees who were attacking Jesus, but the Scriptures show that the Kingdom of God should be on our minds. After all, we are supposed to pray for the Kingdom to come (Matthew 6:10) and Jesus told us to "seek first the kingdom of God and His righteousness" (verse 33).

As we consider how we can have the Kingdom of God as our primary goal and keep it on our minds, we need to understand that the knowledge of this Kingdom is not automatically programmed within us. The popular idea that all the knowledge and wisdom we need is already within us and that all we have to do is look within ourselves to find it is not supported by the Bible.

Our fleshly, human minds are not automatically in sync with God. As our Creator, God knows how we were made. He declares, "The [human] heart is deceitful above all things, and desperately wicked; who can know it?" (Jeremiah 17:9).

The prophet through whom God spoke these words understood what God said. Responding to God, Jeremiah said, "O LORD, I know the way of man is not in himself; it is not in man who walks to direct his own steps" (Jeremiah 10:23).

The way we can transition from our natural human ways of thinking and acting to the way God wants us to be begins with acknowledgment of and repentance of our sins.

When we repent of our sins, are baptized and begin following the lead of the Holy Spirit, we voluntarily place ourselves under the laws and authority of the coming Kingdom of God.

Describing this process, the apostle Paul, who was being held prisoner in Rome at the time, explained, "He [God, the Father] has delivered us from the power of darkness and conveyed us into the kingdom of the Son of His love" (Colossians 1:13). So there is a sense of us being symbolically "conveyed," "translated" (King James Version) or "transferred" (English Standard Version) into the Kingdom when we commit our lives to God and begin living as He instructs.

Our primary allegiance is transferred from all kingdoms of this world to God's Kingdom. We are then subject to different laws (God's laws) and belong to a different community (the Church of God).

The Holy Spirit helps us obey God's laws. This spirit "of power and of love and of a sound mind" (2 Timothy 1:7) gives us the ability to live by God's laws even though we are still human with human weaknesses.

Those who are led by the Spirit of God are called the "sons of God" (Romans 8:14). This same spirit empowers the Church to fulfill its commission. In this sense, we have the opportunity to taste or experience "the powers of the age to come" (Hebrews 6:4-5).

Where is the Kingdom of God and how can we enter it?

Even though the Bible speaks of our "citizenship" as being in heaven after we are baptized (Philippians 3:20), in order to enter the Kingdom of God humans must be changed from flesh and blood into spirit, from mortal into immortal, at Jesus' second coming (1 Corinthians 15:50-53; Hebrews 9:28). When the Kingdom of God comes to Earth, it will rule over all the "kingdoms of this world" (Revelation 11:15).

Unfortunately, in reading Jesus' statement that "the Kingdom of God is within you," many have mistakenly limited the Kingdom of God to a philosophical perspective or a way of thinking. In reality, the coming Kingdom of God is far more than what is in the hearts and minds of Jesus' followers.

In fact, it is the Kingdom that God's faithful elect will enter at Christ's return and that will be established here on Earth.

Chapter Eight

THE VEIL OF DECEPTION

The enemy challenges our right to inherit the things of the Kingdom by taking us back to the things of the law. When the law is the center of our focus, there is a veil over our eyes and we cannot see spiritual truth. We experience condemnation and frustration, which are products of the law, rather than life and peace, which are products of the Spirit. **2 Corinthians 3:6-9; Romans 3:23**

2Co 3:14 But their minds were blinded: for until this day remaineth the same vail untaken away in the reading of the old testament; which vail is done away in Christ.

2Co 3:15 But even unto this day, when Moses is read, the vail is upon their heart.

The Pharisees' focus was on the law and they missed the whole point of the gospel.

Mat 9:13 But go ye and learn what that meant, I will have mercy, and not sacrifice: for I am not come to call the righteous, but sinners to repentance **[a change in the direction of their thinking].**

Mat 12:7 But if ye had known what this meant, I will have mercy, and not sacrifice, ye would not have condemned the guiltless.

The Pharisees were of their father the devil.

John 8:44 Ye are of your father the devil, and the lusts of your father ye will do. He was a murderer from the beginning, and abode not in the truth, because there is no truth in him. When he spoke a lie, he spoke of his own: for he is a liar, and the father of it.

Their doctrine "shut up" the Kingdom and prevented men from entering in.

Mat 23:13 But woe unto you, scribes and Pharisees, hypocrites! For <u>ye shut up the kingdom of heaven against men</u>: for <u>ye neither go in</u> yourselves, <u>neither suffer ye them that are entering to go in.</u>

They lay burdens on people that could not be lifted.

Mat 23:4 For they bind heavy burdens and grievous to be borne, and lay them on men's shoulders; but they themselves will not move them with one of their fingers.

They carried out the "work of their father the devil."

Isa 14:16 They that see thee shall narrowly look upon thee, and consider thee, saying, Is this the man that made the earth to tremble, that did shake kingdoms;

Isa 14:17 That made the world as a wilderness, and destroyed the cities thereof; that opened not the house of his prisoners?

Persecuted for His Name's Sake

*John 15:20 Remember the word that I said unto you, The servant is not greater than his lord. <u>If they have persecuted me</u>, <u>they will also persecute</u> **[to harass or call into question because of one's beliefs, to cause to flee]** <u>you</u>; if they have kept my saying, they will keep yours also.*

Joh 15:21 But all these things will they do unto you <u>for my name's sake</u> **[position of authority]**, *because they know* **[understand]** *not him that sent me.*

Jesus was the "Word made flesh." He was the Son of God. He and His Father were one. It was Jesus' identity or position that He held with His Father that was challenged.

Satan challenged Jesus' right to be called the son of God.
"If you are the son of God, prove it!" **Matthew 3:17; Matthew 4:3 -9**

The Pharisees called it blasphemy when Jesus claimed to be one with His Father. How can you, being a man, say that you are "equal with God"?

> ***John 10:30–33****I and my Father are one. **31** Then the Jews took up stones again to stone him. **32** Jesus answered them, Many good works have I shewed you from my Father; for which of those works do ye stone me? **33** The Jews answered him, saying, For a good work we stone thee not; but for blasphemy; <u>and because that thou, being a man, makes thyself God.</u>*

The Pharisees tried to discredit Jesus by relating His performance to the regulations of the law and to the traditions of the elders.

John 9:16 *Therefore said some of the Pharisees, This man is not of God, because he kept not the sabbath day, How can a man that is a sinner do such miracles?*

Luke 13:14 *Jesus healed the woman who had an infirmity 18 years* ***14*** *And the ruler of the synagogue answered with indignation, because that Jesus had healed on the sabbath day, and said unto the people, There are six days in which men ought to work: in them therefore come and be healed, and not on the sabbath day.*

Matthew 9:2 *And, behold, they brought to him a man sick of the palsy, lying on a bed: and Jesus seeing their faith said unto the sick of the palsy; Son, be of good cheer; thy sins be forgiven thee.****3*** *And, behold, certain of the scribes said within themselves<u>, This man blasphemed</u>.* ***4*** *And Jesus knowing their thoughts said<u>, Wherefore think ye evil in your hearts?</u>* ***<u>5</u>*** <u>*For whether is easier, to say, Thy sins be forgiven thee; or to say, Arise, and walk?*</u>***<u>6</u>*** <u>*But that ye may know that the Son of man hath power on earth to forgive sins*</u>*, (then saith he to the sick of the palsy) Arise, take up thy bed, and go unto thine house.*

Luke 5:21 *And the scribes and the Pharisees began to reason, saying, <u>Who is this which spoke blasphemies? Who can forgive sins, but God alone?</u>*

Matthew 9:9–11V11 *And when the Pharisees saw it, they said unto his disciples, <u>Why ate your Master with publicans and sinners?</u>*

Matthew 9:14 *Then came to him the disciples of John, saying, <u>Why do we and the Pharisees fast oft, but thy disciples fast not?</u>*

Matthew 12:2 *But when the Pharisees saw it, they said unto him, Behold, <u>thy disciples do that which is not lawful to do upon the sabbath day</u>.*

Matthew 12:22–24 *Then was brought unto him one possessed with a devil, blind, and dumb: and he healed him, in so much that the blind and dumb both spoke and saw.**23** And all the people were amazed, and said, Is not this the son of David?**24** But when the Pharisees heard it, they said, <u>This fellow doth not cast out devils, but by Beelzebub</u> the prince of the devils.*

Matthew 15:1–3 Your disciples transgress the traditions of the elders.

Jesus was crucified over the identity issue. How can you, being a man, say you are equal with God?

> ***Mat 26:63** But Jesus held his peace. And the high priest answered and said unto him, I adjure thee by the living God, that thou <u>tell us whether thou be the Christ, the Son of God.</u> **64**<u>Jesus saith unto him, Thou hast said</u>: nevertheless I say unto you, Hereafter shall ye see the Son of man sitting on the right hand of power, and coming in the clouds of heaven. **65** Then the high priest rented his clothes, saying, <u>He hath spoken blasphemy</u>; what further need have we of witnesses? Behold, now ye have heard his blasphemy. **66** What think ye? They answered and said, <u>He is guilty of death.</u>*

John 19:7 We have a law and by our law he is guilty of death.

Leviticus 24:16 Anyone that blasphemes the name of the Lord is guilty of death.

Matthew 27:11 Jesus claimed to be the king of the Jews.

Matthew 27:18 For envy they delivered Him. **Isaiah 14:13-14**

Matthew 27:27-30 The soldiers mocked Him. They dressed him in a crown of thorns, a scarlet robe, and put a reed in his hand.

The crown of thorns represented His works **Genesis 3:18.**

The scarlet robe represented His sins as a man.

The reed was used to mock the scepter of righteousness **Heb 1:8.**

Matthew 27:39-44 If He is the King of Israel, let him save himself!

Matthew 27:46-49 If He is who He says He is, God won't forsake Him.

John 19:19,21 Pilate wrote "Jesus of Nazareth, King of the Jews." The Jews said change it to He said He was the King of the Jews.

Matthew 27:50-54 Truly this was the "Son of God."

When Jesus was challenged, He was not moved because He knew who He was and He embraced it.

We are persecuted and challenged in the same way. We were created in God's image and given dominion over all things. It is that identity that the enemy wants to steal. How can you, being mere men, say you are one with God?

Mat 10:24 *The disciple is not above his master, nor the servant above his lord.*

25 *It is enough for the disciple that he be as his master, and the servant as his lord. If they have called the master of the house Beelzebub, how much more shall they call them of his household?*

Chapter Nine

YOU JUDGE YOURSELVES UNWORTHY

In **Acts 13:33-46** Paul explains that God's Word was first delivered to the Jews. Jesus came and justified them from all things that the law could not justify them from. The Jews were filled with envy and blasphemy and contradicted all that Jesus had done. They judged themselves "unworthy of everlasting life."

***Acts 13:38** Be it known unto you therefore, men and brethren, that through this man is preached unto you the forgiveness of sins:*

***39** And by him all that believe are justified from all things, from which ye could not be justified by the law of Moses.**45** But when the Jews saw the multitudes, they were filled with* *envy, and spoke against those things which were spoken by Paul, contradicting and blaspheming. **46** Then Paul and Barnabas waxed bold, and said, It was necessary that the word of God should first have been spoken to you: but seeing ye put it from you, and judge yourselves unworthy of everlasting life, lo, we turn to the Gentiles.*

They "shut up the kingdom." Their doctrine, according to the law, disqualified them from receiving the things of God. **Matthew 23:4,13, Romans 3:23**

How many times do we "judge ourselves" to be unworthy of everlasting life? The enemy presents us with circumstances and shortcomings and we lose sight of who we really are.

Things That Perish

Christians find themselves searching for anything that will produce a sense of value in their lives because they feel unfulfilled. Without realizing it, they base their sense of value on things of the flesh that are subject to change. Their sense of self-worth comes from their spouses, children, jobs, education, physical assets, achievements etc. The only thing that can really set us free and cause us to feel good about who we are is to begin to see who God created us to be and to get a glimpse of the value that He places on our lives. Jesus was delivered to the cross, not to satisfy God so that He could forgive our sins but to relieve us from the condemnation in the flesh that keeps us from seeing our true identity as His sons and daughters.

Act 4:12 Neither is there salvation in any other: for there is none other name under heaven given among men, whereby we must be saved [delivered from the condemnation that comes from the law].

If our sense of value is based on anything other than what God has done for us, it is subject to change and failure.

Chapter Ten

THE SPIRIT OF INFIRMITY

*Luke 13:11 And, behold, there was a woman which had a spirit of infirmity **[feebleness of body or mind, malady, moral frailty, weakness]** eighteen years, and was bowed together **[to stoop, to be completely overcome by]**, and could in no wise lift up **[unbend, reverse]** herself.*

The spirit of infirmity is associated with intimidation and accusation coming from the adversary over one's inability to overcome a situation. Anytime you are faced with an oppressive situation that you seemingly have no way out of, the lies of the enemy are involved.

Jesus has compassion on people and heals those that are oppressed **[to burden spiritually or mentally]** of the devil.

***Act 10:38** How God anointed Jesus of Nazareth with the Holy Ghost and with power: who went about doing good, and healing all that were oppressed of the devil; for God was with him.*

Where Is God?

***Psa 42:9** I will say unto God my rock, Why hast thou forgotten me? Why do I mourn because of the oppression of the enemy?*

Psa 42:10 As with a sword in my bones, mine enemies reproach me; while they say daily unto me, Where is thy God?

*Psa 42:11 Why art thou cast down, O my soul? And why art thou disquieted **[in great commotion, rage, war, moan]** within me? Hope thou in God: for I shall yet praise him, who is the health of my countenance, and my God.*

The number one thing that the enemy wants to challenge us with is the fact that "God is with us." Have you ever heard the enemy say, "Where is your God now?" He points a finger at God in our circumstances and makes us feel like God has abandoned us, like God does not care, and like God is not helping us because we don't deserve help.

Jesus was able to dispel the lies of the enemy because He was anointed with the Holy Spirit and God was with Him. When we are listening to the voice of the Holy Spirit and we are not moved from the position that "God is with us," we too will be able to dispel the lies of the enemy and we will be able to walk out our seemingly hopeless circumstances in victory.

Chapter Eleven

RECOVERING OUR SIGHT

2Co 3:16 Nevertheless when it shall turn to the Lord, the vail shall be taken away.

2Co 3:17 Now the Lord is that Spirit: and where the Spirit of the Lord is, there is liberty.

2Co 3:18 But we all, with open face beholding as in a glass the glory of the Lord, are changed into the same image from glory to glory, even as by the Spirit of the Lord.

Jesus came to redeem us from the works of the law. When we embrace what He has done for us and allow the Spirit of God to lead us, our eyes are opened to who we are and what we have been called to do.

Moses said, "<u>Unless I know that you are with me, I can not go</u>." **Exodus 33:12-22** Moses said, "Who shall I say has sent me?" God's answer was, "I am." When we begin to get the revelation of the concept that "I am" one with my Father, we too will have the power to open up the doors of the Kingdom to the people of the world.

The Pharisees were of their father the devil and went about disclaiming the things of the Kingdom through the law. They caused people to become slaves to the law and thus produced captives. The Pharisees through his inspiration shut up the gates of the Kingdom so that no one could enter in.

Jesus was of His Father and set the captives free **Acts 10:38**

He brought the Kingdom to the people.

Matthew 4:23 Jesus went about preaching the gospel of the kingdom and healing all manner of sickness and disease.

> *Matthew 9:35-36 And Jesus went about all the cities and villages, teaching in their synagogues, and preaching the gospel of the*

kingdom, and healing every sickness and every disease among the people.

36 But when he saw the multitudes, he was moved with compassion on them, because they fainted, and were scattered abroad, as sheep having no shepherd.

Luke 9:11... He received them, and spoke unto them of the kingdom of God, and healed them that had need of healing.

Jesus brought people to life.

John 5:24 Verily, verily, I say unto you, He that heareth my word, and believeth on him that sent me, hath everlasting life, and shall not come into condemnation; <u>but is passed from death unto life.</u>

25 Verily, verily, I say unto you, The hour is coming, and now is, <u>when the dead shall hear the voice of the Son of God: and they that hear shall live.</u>

The people did not always believe that Jesus and His father were one when He told them, but when He began to demonstrate the things of the Kingdom; the people were filled with awe.

Jesus said, *"Don't believe me because I say I am the son of God. The works that I do will prove that I am the son of God."*

> **Joh 10:36** *Say ye of him, whom the Father hath sanctified, and sent into the world, Thou blasphemes; because I said, I am the Son of God?* ***37*** *If I do not the works of my Father, believe me not.* ***38*** *But if I do, though ye believe not me, believe the works: that ye may know, and believe, that the Father is in me, and I in him.*

Luke 8:25 When Jesus rebuked the wind and water "And they being afraid wondered, saying one to one another, <u>What manner of man is this!</u> For he commanded even <u>the winds and water</u>, and they <u>obey him</u>."

Matthew 27:50-54 Jesus gave up the ghost, the veil was rented, the earth quaked and the centurion and those that were with him said, <u>"Truly this was the son of God."</u>

Matthew 27:11-14 <u>Pilate marveled</u> **[admired]** <u>greatly</u> Jesus when He stood before the governor and the governor asked him if He was the son of God. His reply was, "Thou sayest." When he was accused, He said nothing.

Matthew 9:8 When the man with palsy picked up his bed and walked, "the people marveled that God had given such power to man."

Luke 5:25-26 Jesus healed the man with palsy that was lowered through the ceiling and the people responded ... filled with fear, saying, "We have seen strange things to day."

John 3:2 Nicodemus said, "No one can do these things unless God is with Him."

Luke 19:37 When Jesus made his entry into Jerusalem on a colt....

"The whole multitude of disciples began to rejoice with a loud voice for all the mighty works that they had seen 38 saying, Blessed be the Kings that cometh in the name of the Lord; peace in heaven, and glory in the highest." **40** The Pharisees wanted them rebuked for their loud proclamations but the Scriptures say that if they were not allowed to voice their praises, the stones would cry out in praises!

Luke 7:16 When Jesus raised a widow woman's son from the dead, <u>the people glorified God</u> saying, "<u>God has visited His people.</u>"

Everyone is waiting for an "Immanuel" moment. Who are we that God would visit us? We are ministers of the Spirit that sets people free. **2 Corinthians 3:6**

The whole world is waiting for the sons of God to manifest themselves.

They are waiting for us to boldly assume our identity. We were created in the image of God. Jesus exchanged His life for ours. We are filled with the same glory and honor that Jesus was filled with. We have been given the power to manifest the things of the Kingdom. We have inherited the throne and hold the scepter of righteousness. We and the Father are one!

> ***Rom 8:19*** *For the earnest expectation **[intense anticipation]** of the creature waited for the manifestation of the sons of God.*
>
> *Rom 8:21 Because the creature itself also shall be delivered from the bondage of corruption into the glorious liberty of the children of God.*

Rom 8:22 For we know that the whole creation groaned and travailed in pain together until now.

Jesus said, "As my Father has sent me, so I send you. Receive the Holy Spirit." **John 20:20-21**

Act 10:38 How God anointed Jesus of Nazareth with the Holy Ghost and with power: who went about doing good, and healing all that were oppressed of the devil; for God was with him.

Luke 4:18 The Spirit of the Lord is upon me, because he hath anointed me to preach the gospel to the poor; he hath sent me to heal the brokenhearted, to preach deliverance to the captives, and recovering of sight to the blind, to set at liberty them that are bruised.

Where the Spirit of the Lord is, there is liberty!

***2Co 3:17** Now the Lord is that Spirit: and where the Spirit of the Lord is, there is liberty.*

2Co 3:18 But we all, with open face beholding as in a glass the glory of the Lord, are changed into the same image from glory to glory, even as by the Spirit of the Lord.

Chapter Twelve

SALVATION, THE THEME OF THE GOSPEL

Religion's theme: Confess your sins so God will accept you and give you eternal life. An unholy man can't fellowship with a holy God.

It is very much geared to the concept that God is sin and Commandment conscious. If you don't confess your sins, God will be forced to sentence you to hell. Sin is a violation of the law of Commandments.

Ephesians 1:3–14 We have obtained an inheritance, that we should be to the praise of His glory, after we have heard the word of truth **V13**, the gospel of your salvation.

What is the word of truth about the gospel of our salvation?

Salvation by Definition: rescue, liberty, freedom to experience a Good quality of life.

Rescue from what? Freedom from what?

God's theme is restoration, restoration of man to his God given position and identity as a son of God.

Salvation is the theme of the Gospel. God wants to save us **[rescue, set free]** from the disqualifying condemnation that comes from the enemy.

> ***Psa 106:4*** *Remember me, O LORD, with the favor that thou bearest unto thy people:* ***O visit me with thy salvation; 5 That I may see the good of thy chosen****, that I may rejoice in the gladness of thy nation,* ***that I may glory with thine inheritance.*** *10 And he saved them from the hand of him that hated them, and redeemed them from the hand of the enemy.*

Genesis 1:27–28 God created man in His image and gave him dominion over all of the works of His hands.

Isaiah 14:13–14 Satan is jealous of our position. He wants to be like God. In fact, he wants to exalt himself above God.

Satan's objective is to sever our relationship as a son and joint heir that has been destined to take dominion

> ***Ephesians 6:12*** *For we wrestle not against flesh and blood, but against principalities, against powers, against the rulers of the darkness of this world, against spiritual wickedness in high places.*

Spiritual wickedness in high places (Strong's Dictionary) To corrupt that which is sound; to separate the component parts of a body so it becomes weak.

> ***Ephesians 6:10*** *Finally, my brethren, be strong in the Lord, and in the power of his might. (Amp) In conclusion, be strong in the Lord [be empowered through your union with Him].*

Two opposing seeds:

God speaks concerning His seed and Satan's seed after the garden incident

> *Genesis 3:15 And I will put enmity [opposition] between thee and the woman, and between thy seed and her seed;* **it shall bruise thy head, and thou shalt bruise his heel.**

Thou shalt bruise his heel-(Strong's) *liar in wait*—one who tries to sabotage another's position by underhanded tactics.

Satan is called an angel of light and a wolf in sheep's clothing. **Matthew 7:15; 2 Corinthians 11:14–15**

Adam and Eve lost their sense of identity and the focus was shifted from God to self. When works become the focus of attention, everyone falls short of the glory of God. Condemnation attached to our works says, "You are NOT like God." You do not deserve your inheritance.

God's focus is restoring to us what is rightfully ours. He is going to accomplish that! **[He shall bruise his head Genesis 3:15]**

> *Isaiah 14:24 The LORD of hosts hath sworn, saying, Surely as I have thought, so shall it come to pass; and as I have purposed, so shall it stand: 25 That I will break the Assyrian in my land, and upon my mountains tread him under foot: then*

*shall his yoke depart from off them, and his burden depart from off their shoulders. **26** This is the purpose that is purposed upon the whole earth: and this is the hand that is stretched out upon all the nations. **27** For the LORD of hosts hath purposed, and who shall disannul it? And his hand is stretched out, and who shall turn it back?*

1 John 3:8 *He that committed sin is of the devil; for the devil sinned from the beginning. For this purpose the Son of God was manifested, that he might destroy the works of the devil.*

Acts 26:16-28 *Jesus manifested Himself to Paul for a purpose!*

Acts 26:18 *To open their eyes, and to turn them from darkness to light, and from the power of Satan unto God, that they may receive forgiveness of sins, and inheritance among them, which are sanctified by faith that is in me.*

God's purpose is to destroy the works of the devil so that we can walk in our inheritance. The Old Testament concept concerning the "year of jubilee" presents a type and shadow of this.

> ***Leviticus 25:10*** *And you shall hallow the fiftieth year and proclaim liberty throughout all the land to all its inhabitants. It shall be a jubilee for you; and each of you shall return to his ancestral possession [which through poverty he was compelled to sell], and each of you shall return to his family [from whom he was separated in bond service].*

> ***Ezekiel 46:17*** *But if he gives a gift out of his inheritance to one of his servants, then it shall be his until the year of liberty [the Year of Jubilee]; after that it shall be returned to the prince; only his sons may keep a gift from his inheritance [permanently].* ***18*** *Moreover, the prince shall not take of the people's inheritance by oppression, thrusting them out of their property; what he gives to his sons he shall take out of his own possession, so that none of My people shall be separated from his [inherited] possession.*

God wants to save us so that we can walk in our true identity! We are sons of God, created in the image of our

Father, full of His power and might, destined to rule, reign and to take dominion.

YOU through HIM

Chapter Thirteen

MINISTERS OF THE SPIRIT

The Holy Spirit makes us God conscious. He reveals the position that God intended for us to walk in. He reveals our true identity as sons and daughters created in the image of God destined to take dominion over the works of God's hands. **2 Corinthians 3:16-18**

The Holy Spirit reveals the true character and intent of God the Father and Jesus to us. **John 16:13-16**

John 3:16-17 Jesus came to save not to condemn.

Hebrews 10:15-17 The Holy Spirit writes God's laws **[principles that govern His Kingdom]** in our hearts.

He does not write the law of Commandments.

Romans 7:4-6 All of our connection to the law has been done away with. When it says in Hebrews that the Holy Spirit writes God's laws on our hearts, he is not talking about the law of Commandments.

John 15:10-13 The commandment of the new covenant is to love one another as we have been loved.

The Gospel of the Kingdom does not involve the things of the law.

Matthew 9:12-13, 35-38 The law of the Kingdom is about showing our brothers the mercy and compassion that God has for them. It is not about judgment and sin.

Matthew 10:7-8 Jesus commissions us to do as He has done—heal the sick, raise the dead, cast out devils; freely you have received, freely give.

Acts 10:38 Jesus was anointed with the Holy Spirit and went about healing all that were sick and oppressed of the devil.

Oppressed: to overpower, to exercise dominion against, to cause fear because the consequences of not meeting obligations result in punishment. **[Genesis 3:14-15]**

2 Corinthians 3:6 We are ministers of the Spirit—not ministers of the law.

The Law of Liberty

Ministers of the Spirit minister according to the law of liberty

1 Corinthians 2:1-5 I am determined to know nothing among you save Jesus Christ and Him crucified **[V 2]** that your faith should not stand in the wisdom of men but in the power of God. **[V 5]**

1 Peter 4:8-11 Love covers a multitude of sins, be good stewards of the grace of God that God might be glorified.

James 2

*James 2:1 My brethren, have not the faith of our Lord Jesus Christ, the Lord of glory **[dignity, honor]**, with respect of persons.*

V 2-6 For example: Rich/poor

V 8-9 If you love your neighbor as yourself, you fulfill the law of liberty, but if you have respect of persons, you are guilty of sin and are convinced of the law as transgressors.

V 9 [Mirror] *To judge anyone on the outward appearance is a sin.* **[Sin is anything that robs you of your allotted portion, which is the true measure of your life.]** *This violates the law of liberty and revives condemnation and guilt.*

1 John 4:8 *He that committed sin is of the devil; for the devil sinned from the beginning. For this purpose the Son of God was manifested, that he might destroy the works of the devil.*

V 10-12 If you don't keep the whole law of Commandments you are a transgressor. So also is the law of liberty. **[If you lower the standard of the law in just one aspect, you have failed entirely.]**

Matthew 7:1-2 Judge not that you be not judged. When you judge others, you are brought under the same condemnation that you bring them under.

James 2:14 Faith without works is dead. He is talking about showing others the mercy and compassion of Jesus.

V 13 Mercy overcomes when passing judgment will not. **Romans 2:4**

James 3:8-9 We bless God and curse men, which are made after the similitude of God. This is not right!

1 Peter 2:17 Honor **[value]** all men

1 Timothy 2:1-6 Make supplications, prayers, intercessions and giving of thanks for all men—those in authority—king—for this is good **v4** God would have all men be saved and come to the knowledge of the truth.

> ***AMP1 Timothy 2: 4** Who wishes all men to be saved and [increasingly] to perceive and recognize and discern and know precisely and correctly the [divine] Truth.**6** Jesus gave his life for all to be testified **[evident]** in due time.*

Acts 10:28 God has shown me that I should not call any man common [unholy] or unclean [impure, foul, demonic].

Luke 6:35-37 Children of the Highest show mercy even to their enemies. They are not judgmental.

***Luke 6:35** But love ye your enemies, and do good, and lend, hoping for nothing again; and your reward shall be great, and ye shall be the children of the Highest: for he is kind unto the unthankful and to the evil.*

36 Be ye therefore merciful, as your Father also is merciful.

37 Judge not, and ye shall not be judged: condemn not, and ye shall not be condemned: forgive, and ye shall be forgiven:

Children of the Highest are in love with people. Children of their father the devil love the message of judgment more than they love people. They lay burdens on people that can't be lifted and "shut up the Kingdom." **Matthew 23:4,13,15; John 8:44**

Ephesians 4:22-32 When we judge ourselves or anyone else based on their outside appearance rather than what Jesus has done for them, we grieve the Holy Spirit. We are to put off the "old man's" way of looking at things and put on the new man, which judges everything and everyone in light of the cross. **V 22-24**

When we look at things through the old man mentality, we give place to the devil. **V 27**

***Ephesians 4:29** Let no corrupt communication proceed out of your mouth, but*

> *that which is good to the use of edifying, that it may minister grace unto the hearers.*
>
> ***30** And grieve not the holy Spirit of God, whereby ye are sealed unto the day of redemption.*

Corrupt decaying, separated from its source of life, broken down into its component parts.

God says that we are to minister grace to the hearers and edify them. When we let corrupt communication come out of our mouths we look at others, or ourselves, as though we have no savior. We separate them from their true source of life by focusing on the man rather than on the savior.

What is the divine truth that God wants man to recognize? **Ephesians 1:3–12** We are blessed with all spiritual blessings in Christ Jesus. We have obtained an inheritance as God's sons *"to the praise of His glory."*

Philemon 6 Our faith becomes powerful and active by putting our focus on the power of God in everything and in everyone.

Romans 14 Our purpose is not to pass judgment on everyone based on their beliefs. Everyone must be fully persuaded in their own minds and it is God that holds them up and makes them stand. Our job as ministers of the Spirit is to draw people to the love of God and God will do the rest.

The Kingdom is not about rules and regulations, but it is about experiencing righteousness, peace and joy in the Holy Ghost. **V 17**

Romans 15:1-9 We are to edify one another and bear the infirmities of the weak. We receive one another the way Christ received us. When we do this, God is glorified.

> ***Romans 15:5*** *Now the God of patience and consolation grant you to be like minded one toward another according to Christ Jesus:*
>
> *6 That ye may with one mind and one mouth glorify God, even the Father of our Lord Jesus Christ.*
>
> *7 Wherefore receive ye one another, as Christ also received us to the glory of God.*
>
> *8 Now I say that Jesus Christ was a minister of the circumcision for the truth of God, to confirm the promises made unto the fathers:*

9 *And that the Gentiles might glorify God for his mercy...*

NOW AND FOREVER

Php 2:5 *Let this mind be in you, which was also in Christ Jesus:*

Php 2:6 *Who, being in the form of God, thought it not robbery to be equal with God:*

Php 2:7 *But made himself of no reputation, and took upon him the form of a servant, and was made in the likeness of men:*

Assuming our God-given identity is the theme of the Gospel. We are bone of his bones and flesh of his flesh. We were created in the image of God and given dominion over all things. Although Jesus was God, He came in the flesh to minister the things of the Kingdom unto men. He commissioned us to minister to others in the same manner. We were created to fill the earth with the knowledge of the glory of the Lord.

The Gospel becomes powerfully active in our lives as we come to the correct knowledge about who God is and who we are.

> ***2 Peter 1:3 Amp** For His divine power has bestowed upon us all things that [are requisite and suited] to life and godliness, through the [full, personal knowledge of Him] who called us by and to His own glory and excellence.*

Once the Spirit comes to dwell in our lives, we will never be separated from him again.

> ***1Th 4:17** Then we who are alive and remain shall be caught up together with them in the clouds, to meet the Lord in the air: and so shall we ever be with the Lord.*

As we consider that concept, we need to reconsider our idea about what our life after death will involve. If the message for us now is to see ourselves as one with the Father, just as Jesus is one with the Father, never to be separated from Him again, perhaps our concept of heaven has been distorted by traditions and religion.

Matthew 6:9–10... *Thy will be done on earth as it is in heaven.*

If it is God's will for us to have the mind that we are one with Him here and now, then that same principle will continue in heaven, or in the afterlife. The only difference is that in the afterlife, we will not have a flesh body to oppose the law of God.

> **Rom 8:7** *Because the carnal mind is enmity* **[to oppose, hostile]** *against God: for it is not subject to the law* **[the principles that define His will]** *of God, neither indeed can be.*

The flesh will return to dust, but the Spirit will return to God.

> **Ecc 12:7** *Then shall the dust return to the earth as it was: and the spirit shall return unto God who gave it.*

We came from Him and we are going back to Him.

Eph 1:4 *According as he hath chosen us in him before the foundation of the world, that we should be holy and without blame before him in love:*

We will be given a new name. His name. We will totally assume His identity. It is an identity born out of a relationship.

Rev 2:17 He that hath an ear, let him hear what the Spirit saith unto the churches; To him that overcommit will I give to eat of the hidden manna, and will give him a white stone, and in the stone a new name written, which no man known saving he that received it.

Rev 3:12 Him that overcome will I make a pillar in the temple of my God, and he shall go no more out: and I will write upon him the name of my God, and the name of the city of my God, which is new Jerusalem, which cometh down out of heaven from my God: and I will write upon him my new name.

Second death.

Rev 21:9 And there came unto me one of the seven angels which had the seven vials full of the seven last plagues, and talked with me, saying, Come hither, I will shew thee the bride, the Lamb's wife.

> *Rev 21:10 And he carried me away in the spirit to a great and high mountain, and shewed me that great city, the holy Jerusalem, descending out of heaven from God.*
>
> *Rev 21:11 <u>Having the glory of God</u>: and her light was like unto a stone most precious, even like a jasper stone, clear as crystal.*
>
> *Rev 21:22 And I saw no temple therein: for the Lord God Almighty and the Lamb are the temple of it.*
>
> *Rev 21:23 And the city had no need of the sun, neither of the moon, to shine in it: for the glory of God did lighten it, and the Lamb is the light thereof.*

Jesus and His Father were one.

> **John 1:1** *In the beginning was the Word, and the Word was with God, and the Word was God.*
>
> *John 1:2 The same was in the beginning with God.*

We will be one with the Father in the fullest sense. While we are alive in this body, He is in us. When the flesh body dies, we will return to being "in Him."

1Co 15:47 <u>The first man is</u> *of the earth,* <u>earthy</u>*:* <u>the second man is the Lord from heaven.</u>

1Co 15:48 *As is the earthy, such are they also that are earthy: and as is the heavenly, such are they also that are heavenly.*

1Co 15:49 *And as we have borne the image of the earthy, we shall also bear the image of the heavenly.*

It has been God's plan from the very beginning.

Eph 1:9 *Having made known unto us the mystery of his will, according to his good pleasure which he hath purposed in himself:*

Eph 1:10 That in the dispensation of the fulness of times he might gather together in one all things in Christ, both which are in heaven, and which are on earth; even in him:

Eph 1:11 In whom also we have obtained an inheritance, being predestined according to the purpose of him who worketh all things after the counsel of his own will:

But what about the mansion that He is preparing for me?

> **John 14:2** *In my Father's house are many mansions: if it were not so, I would have told you. I am going to prepare a place for you.*
>
> *John 14:3 And if I go and prepare a place for you, I will come again, and receive you unto myself; that where I am, there ye may be also.*

Jesus was comforting His disciples. He said that He was going to leave them, but that He would prepare a way that would enable them to be with Him where He was. Jesus was always in the presence of His Father because He and His Father were one. Where is the Father's house? It is in us. Jesus was preparing a way for the disciples to continually be in the presence of the Father. He was preparing to send the Holy Spirit to them.

> **John 14:16** *And I will pray the Father, and he shall give you another Comforter, that he may abide with you forever;*

> ***John 14:17*** *Even the Spirit of truth; whom the world cannot receive, because it saw him not, neither knew him: but ye know him; for he dwelleth with you, and shall be in you.*

On that day, the day the Holy Spirit comes to dwell in men, men will know that they are "one with the Father."

> ***John 14:20*** *At that day ye shall know that I am in my Father, and ye in me, and I in you.*

Where is the temple of God? We are the temple of God.

What are the principles of the Kingdom?

> ***Rom 14:17*** *For the kingdom of God is not meat and drink; but righteousness, and peace, and joy in the Holy Ghost.*

Jesus made a way for the disciples to experience the things of the Kingdom **[righteousness, peace and joy in the Holy Ghost]** while they were on Earth. The mansion has already been prepared, and we already have access to it. It is the Holy Spirit that dwells in us [in the Father's house] that gives us a direct connection to the Father and the things of the Kingdom while we are living in the flesh body.

Eph 1:10 *That in the dispensation of the fulness of times he might gather together in one all things in Christ, both which are in heaven, and which are on earth; even in him:*

Eph 1:11 In whom also we have obtained an inheritance, being predestinated according to the purpose of him who worketh all things after the counsel of his own will:

Eph 1:12 That we should be to the praise of his glory, who first trusted in Christ

Eph 1:13 In whom ye also trusted, after that ye heard the word of truth, the gospel of your salvation: in whom also after that ye believed, ye were sealed with that holy Spirit of promise

Eph 1:14 Which is the earnest of our inheritance until the redemption of the purchased possession, unto the praise of his glory.

At this moment, He is "in us." When the flesh body is dissolved, we will once again be "in Him."

2Co 5:1 For we know that if our earthly house of this tabernacle were dissolved, we have a building of God, an house not made with hands, eternal in the heavens.

2Co 5:2 For in this we groan, earnestly desiring to be clothed upon with our house which is from heaven:

2Co 5:3 If so be that being clothed we shall not be found naked.

2Co 5:4 For we that are in this tabernacle do groan, being burdened: not for that we would be unclothed, but clothed upon, that mortality might be swallowed up of life.

2Co 5:5 Now he that hath wrought us for the selfsame thing is God, who also hath given unto us the earnest of the Spirit.

2Co 5:6 Therefore we are always confident, knowing that, whilst we are at home in the body, we are absent from the Lord:

There is coming a day, when the spirit returns to the Spirit, that we will clearly see who we are.

> ***1Co 13:12** For now we see through a glass, darkly; but then face to face: now I know in part; but then shall I know even as also I am known.*

> ***1Jn 3:2** Beloved, now are we the sons of God, and it doth not yet appear what we shall be: but we know that, when he shall appear, we shall be like him; for we shall see him as he is.*

Jesus was the Word, and the Word was God and the Word was with God.

As Jesus is, so are we in this world, and in the world to come!

YOU through HIM

SUMMARY

IN ORDER TO BE LIKE JESUS, WE NEED TO ACT THE WAY HE DID AND MAKE THE SAME CHOICES HE WOULD HAVE MADE.

We often hear people say that we need to be more like Christ. This is definitely a good goal to have, but it can be difficult to understand what it actually means. If we stop and think about it for a moment, we might realize that the standards we are holding ourselves to are impossible to reach. Instead of trying to be perfect, we should focus on HIM and not worry about being perfect. I'm not saying we shouldn't try to be more Christ-like, I'm just saying it doesn't mean what we are typically implying.

The closest thing you will find in Scripture about being more like Jesus is in Ephesians 5:1, which says,

THEREFORE BE IMITATORS OF GOD AS DEAR CHILDREN.

Being more like Christ means that you don't have to worry about sin or being disciplined; Jesus took care of all of that already! This means that, no matter what you do, God will still love you. But when you realize that nothing can separate you from God's love, it will change the way you act....

When the apostle Paul says to imitate God, he means that we should wake up to the truth of God's love. The next verse says that this is what God wants us to do!

AND WALK IN LOVE, AS CHRIST ALSO HAS LOVED US AND GIVEN HIMSELF FOR US, AN OFFERING AND A SACRIFICE TO GOD FOR A SWEET-SMELLING AROMA.
EPHESIANS 5:2

The word Paul uses for love in this verse is agape, which is the love of God. This kind of love is different from the love we feel for others, because it is based on how God feels about us, not on what we have done. When we walk in this kind of love, the things that used to make us happy will no longer be appealing, because we are acknowledging the spirit of God inside of us.

If you want to be like Christ, it starts with how you treat others. Acknowledge who your Father is and your identity in Christ, and you will start to see a change in yourself!

Do you want to be more like Christ? Christ was always kind and loving to sinners, tax collectors, and prostitutes. He never separated Himself from them or waited for them to change before He showed them love.

God loves us just the way we are, and His love gives us the power to change.

I agree that we need to be more like Christ, but how do we get there? It's a change that happens when we understand how much God loves us. It's His goodness that leads us to real life change. (Romans 2:4)!

Let's walk in God's love today, and let it fill up every part of our lives.

A NEW COMMANDMENT I GIVE TO YOU, THAT YOU LOVE ONE ANOTHER; AS I HAVE LOVED YOU, THAT YOU ALSO LOVE ONE ANOTHER.

JOHN 13:34

HE WHO DOES NOT LOVE DOES NOT KNOW GOD, FOR GOD IS LOVE.

1 JOHN 4:8

ABOUT THE AUTHOR

Rev, Dr. Georgette J Milbin is a native of Port-au-Prince, Haiti, WI. She studied at the Coconut Creek Atlantic vocational school in Florida, and CCRI College in Rhode Island. She earned her Master's in Business Administration and Theology studies at Charis Bible College, Atlanta.

She then earned her Doctorate in Theology and Religion Philosophy in Christian counseling at RTS. She is also a certified Temperament Counselor, a member of NCCA, and a certified chaplain member of ACA. She is an author, teacher, spiritual leader, business owner, and motivational speaker.

As an effective communicator of God's Word, Dr. Georgette is widely known for her practical and dynamic teaching style, which helps people apply the timeless truths of Scripture to everyday lives. She was a volunteer for a number of years at Team Jesus Ministry where she conducted worship and ministered to inmates in Henry County Jail in Georgia.

She is the founder of AGM Christian Ministries based in Forest Park, Georgia. She also has ministries in Haiti and the Dominican Republic, where she conducts volunteer work mission trips annually. She and her husband, Abner, have been married since 1992. They are the proud parents of five children, three girls and two boys.

SPONSORS

AGM Christian Ministries is a special place where people can come together to learn about Jesus and be part of a friendly group. We want everyone to feel welcomed and loved. We think it's important to create a place where people can really get to know Jesus, find their own special talents, and use them to make God happy. Come join us on Sundays! please call 404-994-6222 for more info.

www.agmchristianministries.org

GAM Travel connects people to the world by providing an exceptional travel experience. We provide personalized, detail-oriented, leisure, cruises travel etc... call 678-842-4283

La Joie personal Home Care At La Joie Personal Home Care, nothing matters more than your health and wellbeing. Since 2000, we've been there for our clients as a comprehensive, friendly and professional Home Care Agency. We shape our caregiving services based on what our clients, and their health professionals, want and need. Get in touch and see what we can do for you or your family members today.

www.lajoiepersonalhomecare.com

Will be a place where our you and our youth will be accepted, loved, taught, cared for and nurtured in the Word God

Wisdom Coaching helps people become the better version of themselves. Please call 678-842-4283 for more info.

YOUR STAR
PRIVATE HOME CARE

Your STAR Private Home CareFeel better in the comfort of your own home. We specialize in Home Care daily or living assistance to an array of individuals. Whether you need daily or weekly assistance due to aging, illness, recovery, or rehabilitation, our care givers will provide an individualized service that you can trust. www.yourstarprivatehomecare.com

BOOK YOUR EVENT. Great service, delivery was right on time. They're very professional and guests loved the throne chair.

www.ryotteevents.com

Made in the USA
Columbia, SC
06 May 2023